Pontius Pilate

and the

Crucifixion of Christ

By William Malicoat

ISBN: 978-1-78364-516-9

www.obt.org.uk

****

THE OPEN BIBLE TRUST
Fordland Mount, Upper Basildon,
Reading, RG8 8LU, UK.

Pontius Pilate
and the Crucifixion of Christ

Contents

Pontius Pilate

Purpose of this first study

Pontius Pilate

Purpose of this first study

This first study is concerned with determining who Pontius Pilate was. There is very little information concerning him either in Scripture or in written history. In knowing who Pilate was, we should gain a greater understanding of the motives and actions that led to the crucifixion of our Lord and Saviour, Jesus Christ. In undertaking this study we will examine the accounts in the synoptic Gospels culminating in the passion as recorded in John's Gospel, thereby giving us a clearer picture of events.

Pilate's Background and character

First, the name Pontius Pilate has much to say about who he was as an individual. It tells us about the location of his family's origin as the name 'Pontius' indicates he was from a region in Southern Italy and that he was from a famous Samnite family and of the tribe of Pontii. Prior to

Pilate's birth, the Samnites were in perpetual war with the Romans. His surname, or cognomen Pilatus, is indicative of a branch of gens (the line of descent through the father) Pontius. It carries a significant meaning: armed with a pilum – a spear or javelin.[1] In Latin Pileatus means wearing the pileus, a cap or badge of a manumitted slave – a freedman, former slave; or the descendant of a freedman.[2]

Second, Pilate was a soldier. He held the rank of *Eques Romanus* – belonging to the knights. In the Roman Army he belonged to the equestrian knights, an equite – a horseman. This would be equal to a general in the American cavalry of the 19th century. In civilian life, the knights were

---

[1] Rusty Russel. "Fallen Empires: Archaeological Discoveries and the Bible." Rusty Russel. http://www.bible-history.com/empires/pilate.html (accessed Oct. 10, 2010)

[2] Rit Nosostro. "Pontius Pilate: Reigned 26 -36 AD, Roman Politician Who Handed Jesus Over to be Crucified." HyperHistory.net. http://www.hyperhistory.net/apwh/bios/b1pilate.html

distinguished from senators, yet wielding much political power.

Most likely Pilate was (an assumption based on this history) a first or second generation removed from a former slave. He had worked his way through the Legions to become a very powerful general. This led him to an appointment as a prefect, or governor. Historically, many high ranking military leaders became governors of a conquered territory.

Third, Pilate was appointed prefect of Judea in the 15th year of Tiberius' reign.[3] It is still being debated as to when the 15th year actually was, and when Pilate actually took control of Judea. Some scholars say Pilate's term began in 25 AD when he was appointed and others say in 26 AD when he physically arrived on the scene. Pilate's headquarters was in Caesarea, but he was in Jerusalem with a token garrison to maintain order during the Passover.

---

[3] Ibid

Jesus was in Jerusalem for the Passover

Jesus, as was the custom of the Jews, went to Jerusalem for the annual Passover celebration. However, He was there for more than just the Passover! He was there to become a living sacrifice ... He knew this in advance of arriving (John 13:1).

Jesus would also hold a final meal with His disciples and would make two significant predictions:

1) He would be betrayed by one of His disciples (John 13:11, 21) and
2) Another of His disciples, Peter, would deny him three times (John 13:38).

During the meal, Satan had already entered into the mind of Judas to hand Jesus over to the Sanhedrin (John 13:2). While they were at the table, Jesus stated He would be betrayed, and even Judas (His betrayer) asked "Is it I?" (Matthew

26:25). Judas shortly thereafter, left the upper room.

Furthermore, in a discourse with Peter Jesus says, "Before the cock crows three times you will deny me" (Matthew 26:34,69-75). Later that night when Judas did betray Him, Jesus asked, "Judas, would you betray the Son of Man with a kiss?" (Luke 22:48).

The Betrayal and Trials of Jesus

Purpose of this second study

The Betrayal and Trials of Jesus

Purpose of this second study

This second study is focused on the betrayal and trials of Jesus. Essentially, Pilate attempted to release Jesus since he found no reason to crucify Him. In the process we will see:

- a conspiracy taking place.
- our Lord and Saviour betrayed by one of His own, and
- three denials by another.

We will also see the fear of those who sought to kill Jesus in the arrest. We will discover the identity of the accusers, what their accusations were, and their motives for wanting Jesus dead.

Furthermore, we will hopefully gain a greater understanding of the soldier who was trapped into crucifying Jesus.

Behind the scenes

Behind the scenes a plot was taking place. The chief priests and the elders were looking for a way to kill Jesus (Matthew 26:3-4; John 11:47-53). They found their man in Judas Iscariot, who agreed to deliver Jesus to them for a mere 30 pieces of silver (Matthew 26:14-16; Mark 14:10-11; Luke 22:4-6).

Knowing the habits of Jesus (John 18:2), Judas planned to betray Him in the Garden of Gethsemane (Matthew 26:36; Mark 14:32). Jesus often went to the garden to rest, to pray and to teach His disciples as it was a quiet and out of the way place where Jesus could find private moments for such things. Jesus felt safe there among the olive trees and gardens of the wealthy and affluent. Jesus probably had a key to the gate and permission from one of His wealthy followers to go there just for those purposes.[4] In the garden,

---

[4] William Barclay. *The Gospel of John*. Vol. 2. Second Edition. (Philadelphia, Pa.: Westminster Press. 1956) 259.

Jesus could camp safely as the garden was peaceful and very private.

Late at night Judas arrived with some officials sent from the high priests and Pharisees, together with a detachment of soldiers, carrying lanterns, torches and weapons (John 18:3). These soldiers would be the Jewish Temple guard[5] under the authority of the chief priests and the Sanhedrin.

According to John this detachment of armed men feared Jesus so much they fell to their knees when He confronted them at the gate and asked them who they were looking for. They answered, "Jesus of Nazareth," Jesus replied, "I am he." Can you imagine, soldiers armed to the hilt, and ready for a battle, being so bowled over by those words and being so afraid of a single unarmed man that they fell back and onto their knees? The power of Christ is immeasurable!

---

[5] William Barclay states that there were Roman soldiers there also, but this is not likely because up to this point the Romans had not been involved. Ibid, 222.

Pontius Pilate and the Crucifixion of Christ 17

The Accusers

Who were these men, the accusers of Jesus? The Sanhedrin, chief priests: Annas, Caiaphas, Datum, Gamaliel, Judas, Levi, Naphthalim, Alexander, Cyrus, and others.[6]

Annas was chief of the Sanhedrin and it was to him in that office that Christ was *first* brought[7] (John 18:13); Annas was a very wealthy and powerful man. His family had controlled the temple and the office of high priest for several generations. Annas not only had a monopoly on the priesthood… having four sons, and a son-in-law (Caiaphas) that had held the office of high priest, but also a monopoly on preapproved victims for holy rituals held in the temple.[8]

---

[6] The Gospel of Nicodemus, 1:1

[7] Adam Clark. *Adam Clarke's 1810/1825 commentary and critical notes on the Bible.* 1825.

[8] William Barclay. *The Gospel of John.* Vol. 2. Second Edition. (Philadelphia, Pa.: Westminster Press. 1956) 264-265.

Caiaphas was high priest and the son-in-law of Annas. According to John, Jesus was first taken to Annas' house (John 18:13). This was done probably as a mark of respect, Annas having been high priest. But possibly for prudence, as Annas was capable of advising his son-in-law in a difficult case. The Saviour was detained there until the chief priests and elders were assembled (Matthew 26:57).[9] Caiaphas was the one that suggested that it would be better for one man (Jesus) to die in order to save the nation of Israel (John 18:14).

Gamaliel was the president of the council. Also known as Rabban Gamaliel the first; commonly, by way of distinction, also called Rabban Gamaliel the elder. He was president of the council after the death of his own father, Rabban Simeon, who was the son of Hillel ... Gamaliel was Paul's master, and the 35th receiver of the traditions, and on this account might not be improperly termed *nomodidaskalos*, a doctor of

[9] Adam Clark. *Adam Clarke's 1810/1825 commentary and critical notes on the Bible.* 1825

the law[10] (Acts 5:34; 22: 3). It is also known that Gamaliel had been the teacher of Saul of Tarsus, the apostle Paul (Acts 22:3).

There were also many other unnamed accusers[11] from the Sanhedrin, Pharisees and other council members, all bearing false witness during the trials of Jesus. Many of them had gathered at the home of Annas and were later found at Caiaphas's residence where others also assembled. By early morning they had moved to Pilate's palace, then onto Herod's and back again. After many hours, the trial finally ended in the death sentence of Jesus, His crucifixion and His death before sunset.

The accusations

The accusations were blasphemy, claiming to be the Christ, the Son of God (Matthew 26:65; Mark 14:64), and declaring Himself to be the King of the Jews (Luke 23:2), attempting to dissolve the Sabbath and overthrow the laws of the fathers,[12]

---

[10] Ibid
[11] The Gospel of Nicodemus, 1:1
[12] Ibid, 1:2

and finally attempting to incite a riot and overthrow the Roman government.

Exactly what is blasphemy? The two definitions we are interested in are the Scriptural definition and the modern English definition.

> 1) Scriptural *blasphemos:* vilification (especially against God): evil speaking, railing.

> 2) Modern English, blas'phemy, n.
>   a) an indignity offered to God by words or writing; reproachful, contemptuous or irreverent words uttered impiously against Jehovah.
>   b) Blasphemy is an injury offered to God, by denying that which is due and belonging to him, or attributing to him that which is not agreeable to his nature.[13]

---

[13] Noah Webster. *Noah Webster's 1828 Dictionary of American English.* 1828

The Trials

In His three year ministry, Jesus made many enemies. A handful of officials, Judas Iscariot and a detachment of soldiers delivered Jesus (John 18:12-13) to the house of the devil himself, Annas. This former high priest was the owner[14] of the businesses Jesus had cleansed from the temple. This man had the biggest axe to grind. He was the leader of the pack and Christ's chief accuser.

The charges were all false. There was no evidence that Jesus blasphemed God. Even the demons called Jesus the Son of God (Matthew 8:29; Mark 5:7; Luke 4:41) because even the demons knew and recognized who Jesus was.

Jesus was delivered to the house of Annas, where Annas gloated. Jesus was then sent to Caiaphas' house. An unspecified time passed as they apparently waited for the council to assemble. A kangaroo court ensued and all of the Jewish justice

---

[14] William Barclay. *The Gospel of John*. Vol. 2. Second Edition. (Philadelphia, Pa.: Westminster Press. 1956) 226

system was violated (Mark 14:55). As early morning approached and the day began, Jesus was bound and delivered to Pilate (Matthew 27:2; Mark 15:1).

Pilate questioned Jesus about the charges and found no fault in Him (Luke 23:4). He discovered Jesus was a Galilean and, since Herod was king over Galilee and knowing Herod was in town for the Passover, decided Jesus should come under the jurisdiction of Herod. Pilate, in an attempt to avoid dealing with this issue, sent Jesus to Herod (Luke 23:6-7).

Herod, having heard of Jesus' many miracles, was very eager to see him, and hoped he would see Jesus perform a miracle for him (Luke 23:8). Not only did Jesus decline to perform a miracle for Herod, He did not even speak to Him. He also refused to defend Himself against the accusations of the Sanhedrin (Luke 23:9). Because Jesus chose to remain mute, Herod had Him clothed in elaborate garments and mocked Him before returning Him to Pilate (Luke 23.11).

Since the Jews had no legal authority to carry out the death penalty, the *ius gladii*, the right of the sword, they had to have the Roman government do it.[15]

Jesus had been returned to Pilate by Herod. In the account of John 18:28-39, Pilate is evidently growing weary with the Jewish leadership. He attempted several times to release Jesus (Matthew 27:15; Mark 15:6; Luke 23:16; John 18:39). Also, we see Pilate almost pleading with Jesus to defend himself and telling Jesus he alone had the power to release Him or have Him crucified (John 19:10). Jesus responded by telling Pilate he had no authority but what God had given him. He knew that prophecy was to be fulfilled. He had to suffer at the hands of the Romans (Matthew 20:18-19). Attempting to appease the crowd, Pilate had Jesus scourged … this was to no avail. Still Pilate argued with the crowd which, by nearly noon, included the Sanhedrin who skillfully worked the crowd to frenzy, insisting the Romans crucify Jesus.

---

[15] Ibid, 272-273.

Pilate could not win, even though he knew Jesus was innocent. He was in a difficult position and didn't really want to condemn an innocent man to death. On the other hand, however, if he released Jesus he risked having a riot on his hands. Pilate attempted to have Herod (a Jewish king) deal with the issue, but that failed and Jesus was returned to him. Next he tried to release Jesus because it was a tradition to release a prisoner at the Passover, which also failed. Then Pilate tried to appease the crowd by having Jesus scourged … that too, failed.[16] Finally, Pilate gave in, washing his hands in the belief that this would absolve him of the responsibility (Matthew 27:24). The one thing Pilate didn't do was "put his foot down and tell the Jews he would have nothing to do with their evil machinations." (Barclay, 277)

---

[16] Ibid, 276-277

The Effects of Pilate's Actions

Purpose of the third study

The Effects of Pilate's Actions

Purpose of the third study

To gain an understanding of Pilate's actions and what were the effects of those actions, in both the immediate term and the long range. For Christianity to be what it is today Pilate's actions had to be the ones he took ... from a human point of view, prophecy would not have been fulfilled, the Law would not have been fulfilled and would not have been abolished, and we would have no Saviour, no sanctification and no redemption.

Pilate made a decision

Pilate gave in to the Jewish leaders; he let them have their way and sent Jesus to be crucified.

Did Pilate fear an insurrection in the middle of the Passover celebration or did he simply want to please the crowd (Matthew 27:24; Mark 15:15)?

Or was he afraid of what might get back to Caesar (John 19:12)? Did washing his hands absolve him of his part in the death of Jesus?

It may be an eternity before the answers to such questions can be known. The one thing we do know is that, because of Pilate's decision, Jesus died a horrible and painful death on the cross at Calvary.

The Crucifixion

After being mocked, scourged, forced to carry His cross through the streets of Jerusalem half-clad and crucified … Jesus then died. By noon Jesus had been nailed to the cross and God began to show His displeasure with the treatment of His Son; darkness came over the land and it remained dark until late that afternoon (Matthew 27:51-53; Mark 15:33; Luke 23:44). At about the ninth hour (Matthew 27:46-50; Mark 15:33-37; Luke 23:46; John 19:30), roughly three o'clock in the afternoon, Jesus gave up the spirit and, as far as Pilate was concerned, passed into Roman history as just another criminal that Rome executed.

However, at the moment of Jesus' death the veil of the temple was rent (*schidzo*: to split or sever)[17] from top to bottom. Also, there was an earthquake and rocks were divided, tombs were opened and bodies were raised (Matthew 27:52). From that moment on a change began to take place in the way God would deal with man. However, fulfillment of prophecy concerning God's Son, Jesus, was not yet completed. It was just beginning.

The Resurrection

Three days on the Jewish calendar passed. As far as we know, Pilate never saw Jesus again either in physical or spiritual form, but we know two more commands of Pilate which concerned Jesus. One was to give Christ's body to Joseph of Arimathaea for burial, and the other was to station guards at the tomb, to seal it and to watch over it as requested by the chief priests.

---

[17] William E. Vine. *Vine's Expository Dictionary of New Testament Words*. (Marmora, New Jersey: Barbour Publishing, Incorporated, 1985)

On the third day Mary Magdalene, Mary (the mother of James and Joses) and Salome (the wife of Zebedee) came with spices to anoint the body of Jesus, but when they got there the stone had been rolled away from the opening of the tomb and the body had gone (Matthew 28:1-6; Mark 16:1-6; Luke 24:1-3; John 20:1). About twilight, angels appeared and the guards were shaken and thrown into a blackout.[18] They rolled the stone away from the tomb and when the women arrived the angels gave them instructions to report to the disciples and have them meet Jesus in Galilee. It was the first day of the week.

Prophecy is fulfilled

"Into thy hand I commend my spirit: Thou hast redeemed me, O Jehovah, thou God of truth" (Psalm 31:5). On the cross Jesus made the statement "Into thy hand I commend my spirit" and died (Luke 23:46). As Isaiah had prophesied in chapter 53 Jesus was the suffering servant;

---

[18] Albert Barnes, *Barnes' Notes On The New Testament* (Grand Rapids: Kregal Publications, 1962) 143.

Jesus was despised and rejected by the chief priests and Jewish leaders; Jesus bore the sins of many, and carried the grief and sorrow of men, He was wounded for our transgressions and iniquities; He was obedient to the cross and remained silent to the death. Jesus became the final blood sacrifice for sins; He fulfilled the Law and ushered in a new era in God's plan for man. The Law was fulfilled in Christ's death and suffering (Luke 24:44-47), and it was later to be abolished (Ephesians 2:14-15; Colossians 2:14-16).

An era ends and a new one begins

With the death, resurrection and ascension of Christ, God changed His way of dealing with man. God, knowing the legal requirements He had placed on Israel were impossible to keep and the blood sacrifices of animals only covered sin temporarily, Christ came to redeem His people. Following His one sacrifice for sin and His resurrection, God again presented the kingdom to Israel. They had rejected Christ Himself and now they were to reject the ministry of the Apostles.

They rejected the kingdom offer because it was not what they were expecting from the Messiah. They were looking for a strong, powerful king to establish an earthly kingdom, to defeat the enemies and occupiers of their land. While, they were not expecting a personal redeemer, that is exactly what they got.

A new administration

During the Acts period Christianity was in its infancy; the disciples were being shown many things, but the disciples ministered mostly to the tribes of Israel (Matthew10:5-6). But God had a bigger plan and Jesus revealed Himself to a zealous young Pharisee (Saul of Tarsus) who would become the Apostle to the Gentiles (Acts 22:21; Romans 11:13; Galatians 2:8; Ephesians 3:8; 1 Timothy 2:7; 2 Timothy 1:11). He would use Saul to lay the groundwork for a new administration of God's plans and purposes … Saul became the Apostle Paul. Furthermore, Paul would later reveal a new administration, a mystery (secret) which had been hidden in God through the ages and revealed only through Paul (Ephesians 3:8-12; Colossians 1:24-28).

A change in covenant

Since Jesus died on the cross, He was given a better ministry and became the mediator of a better covenant. Israel was unable to follow God's first covenant made with their fathers (Hebrews 8:6-13) and that old covenant was "ready to vanish away" (Hebrews 8:13).

God now brought Gentiles into His plan. Initially they were second to Israel (Romans 1:16; 2:9-10), but later He placed them on equal ground with the Jews (Ephesians 3:6).

The Jews had rejected Him time and time again. They lost their spirituality and had become legalistic making the traditions and interpretations of God's law more important than their personal relationship with Him. They had distorted the meaning of the Law and made it of no effect (Matthew 15:6). For all intents and purposes they rendered the covenant of circumcision useless.

The Law became dead rituals and circumcision became nothing more than symbolism. They hardened their hearts and became blind and deaf, and so God's salvation was sent to the Gentiles (Acts 28:25-28).

From law to grace

The abolition of the Law did not give people the license to sin. However, it did free them from the bondage of the Law. Christ's shed blood replaced the blood sacrifices of animals which only covered sin. He gave true redemption and justification through faith in all who believed in Christ as their Saviour (Romans 6).

Conclusion

Conclusion

It may be asked, what do studies two and three have to do with the character of Pontius Pilate, as all that is known and assumed about him was addressed in the first one? Actually both of those studies are very pertinent to the character of Pontius Pilate. Could another have taken Pilate's place? Would we have seen the same results? The answers to those questions would be pure speculation. Would John F. Kennedy be any less dead had someone other than Lee Harvey Oswald shot him November 23, 1963? Did Oswald really kill him? That is still being debated today, nearly 50 years later.

One thing is certain however, there is no debate about whether Pilate had Jesus crucified. It is known to be a fact of human history as it is written in Roman history. He was there as one era was ending and another beginning. Perhaps we should thank God for Pontius Pilate. Without knowing it, He did his part in bringing about a change in God's dealing with mankind.

We must believe in the Word God has given us; regardless of the individuals involved. God gave us the exact persons He required to complete His mission. Pilate, although he was merely a soldier attempting to do his duties, was the perfect character; he fitted God's purposes (Acts 4:27). Whether washing his hands sufficed to absolve him from his part I would very much doubt, but we will never know. Nevertheless, humanly speaking, without Pilate we would not have had a crucified Saviour and may not have had Christianity, and it certainly would not be as we know it today.

Bibliography

Bibliography

Barclay, William. *The Gospel of John*. Vol. 2. Second Edition. Philadelphia, Pa.: Westminster Press. 1956

Barnes, Albert. *Barnes' Notes On The New Testament*. Edited by Rev. Ingram Cobbin. Grand Rapids, Mi.: Kregal Publications. 1962

Buttrick, George A. *The Interpreter's One-Volume Commentary*. Fifteenth Edition. Nashville, TN.: Abingdon Press. 1971

Carter, Warren. *Pontius Pilate: Portraits of a Roman Governor*. Collegeville, Mn.: Liturgical Press. 2003

Clarke, Adam. *The New Testament of our Lord and Saviour Jesus Christ*.[19] Royal Octavo Stereotype Edition. New York, New York: J. Emory and B. Waugh. 1831

---

[19] AKA, Adam Clarke's 1810/1825 commentary and critical notes on the Bible

Eiselen, Frederick Carl, Edwin Lewis, David G. Downey, Eds. *The Abindon Bible Commentary*. New York, New York: Abingdon-Cokesbury Press. 1929

Keck, Leander E., et al, eds. *The New Interpreter's Bible*. Vol. VIII. Nashville, Tn.: Abingdon Press. 1995

Vine, William E. *Vine's Expository Dictionary of New Testament Words*. Marmora, New Jersey: Barbour Publishing, Incorporated, 1985

Webster, Noah. *Noah Webster's 1828 Dictionary of American English*. Springfield, Mass: G. &C. Meriam. 1828

The Gospel of Nicodemus
http://www.bible-history.com/empires/pilate.html
http://www.hyperhistory.net/apwh/bios/b1pilate.html

Also on this subject

Also on this subject

When was Christ's Death and Resurrection?
Peter John-Charles

One might say … as the death, burial and resurrection of our Lord Jesus Christ is annually remembered and celebrated by Christians throughout the world … that far out-weighs details of times and dates.

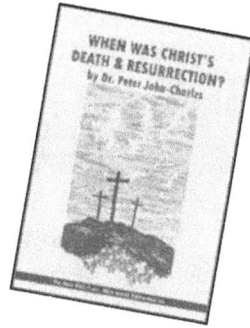

However, any such reaction will quickly be dispelled. Through painstaking application of Scripture, and his good grasp of the Jewish calendar, the author shows that the traditional time-scale of these events is untenable, and puts forward one which harmonises more closely with the biblical record.

The great value in all this is discovering just how perfectly the Lord Jesus Christ fulfilled the types and shadows contained in the Law and the Prophets.

Seemingly dull Levitical ritual bursts into life as we appreciate more fully its wondrous significance in pointing to Israel's Messiah and our Saviour. Sadly, the inaccurate traditional time-table hides much of this edifying truth … truth designed by God as confirmation of the great work of redemption accomplished by our Lord Jesus Christ.

If there is no resurrection of the dead ... what then?

By Charles Ozanne

What is the most distinctive, attractive, and far-reaching doctrine that Christians believe? For the author the answer is the resurrection.

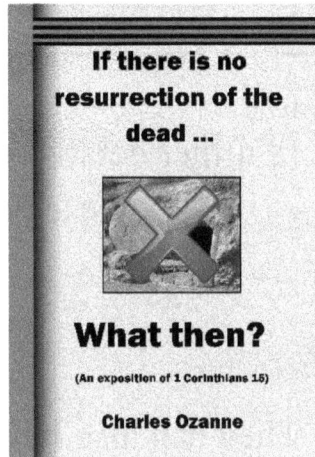

Though not exclusively Christian, since both Judaism and Islam have a doctrine of resurrection of their own, it is nevertheless the most distinctive of all Christian beliefs, and certainly the founder of no other religion claims to have risen from the dead.

It is the most attractive because it holds out the promise of eternal life on the other side of the grave. And it is the most far-reaching because the resurrection life goes on for ever and ever!

That is why 1 Corinthians 15 is such an important chapter. This chapter tackles the whole subject of resurrection against the backdrop of some who denied or doubted there was any such thing. To the Greek way of thinking bodily resurrection was a ludicrous idea, and there were Jews also, the Sadducees in particular (Acts 23:8), who entertained the same scepticism.

Further details of all the books mentioned on these pages can be seen on

www.obt.org.uk

They can also be ordered from that website and also from:

The Open Bible Trust,
Fordland Mount, Upper Basildon,
Reading, RG8 8LU, UK.

They are also available as eBooks from Amazon and Apple
and as KDP paperbacks from Amazon.

About the author

William Malicoat was born in Dallas, Texas, in 1950 and attended Eisenhower High School in Lawton Oklahoma. On leaving school he enlisted in the United States Marine Corps and served a one year tour in the Republic of Vietnam in 1969. He accepted Christ as his Lord and Saviour in 1987 and attended Grace Bible College of Grand Rapids, Michigan, graduating with a Bachelor of Religious Education. Later he attended Cameron University of Lawton, Oklahoma, graduating with a Master of Science in Psychology. He became a Licensed Professional Counselor and worked in the mental health field for several years before retiring. At present he lives in Mountain Park, Oklahoma, with his wife and daughter.

About this book

Pontius Pilate
And the Crucifixion of Christ

Here we have not only a pen-portrait of the most well-known of all Roman Governors, but also an account of the betrayal and trials of Jesus Christ, culminating in his trial before Pontius Pilate.

The author also considers the effect Pilate's actions had on the course of history.

Publications of The Open Bible Trust must be in accordance with its evangelical, fundamental and dispensational basis. However, beyond this minimum, writers are free to express whatever beliefs they may have as their own understanding, provided that the aim in so doing is to further the object of The Open Bible Trust. A copy of the doctrinal basis is available on **www.obt.org.uk** or from:

THE OPEN BIBLE TRUST
Fordland Mount, Upper Basildon,
Reading, RG8 8LU, UK.